Lady Katherine Grey: A Tudor Prisoner

A Tudor Times Insight

By Tudor Times

Published by Tudor Times Ltd

Tudor Times Insights

Tudor Times Insights are books collating articles from our website www.tudortimes.co.uk which is a repository for a wide variety of information about the Tudor and Stewart period 1485 – 1625. There you can find material on People, Places, Daily Life, Military & Warfare, Politics & Economics and Religion. The site has a Book Review section, with author interviews and a book club. It also features comprehensive family trees, and a 'What's On' event list with information about forthcoming activities relevant to the Tudors and Stewarts.

Titles in the Series

Profiles

People

Politics & Economy

Contents

Lady Katherine Grey: Tudor Prisoner

Introduction

Lady Katherine Grey is very little known compared with her older sister, Lady Jane, yet her life in many ways encapsulated the problems of the Tudor succession, and the difficulties that almost everyone of royal blood encountered.   First, a pawn in the plans of the Duke of Northumberland, and then disliked and distrusted by Elizabeth I, she sought to find happiness in marriage, but suffered imprisonment and separation from her husband.

Katherine's life was lived in the east and south of England, in the houses of the nobility and gentry in the country and the grand town houses and palaces of London, including that most dreaded of fortresses, the Tower of London.

Part 9   contains Lady Katherine Grey's Life Story and articles 'following in [her] footsteps'. Katherine's life was defined by her royal blood. As a potential heir to the crown in a country riven with dynastic and religious uncertainty, her life was not her own.

Family Tree

Lady Katherine GREY
Countess of Hertford

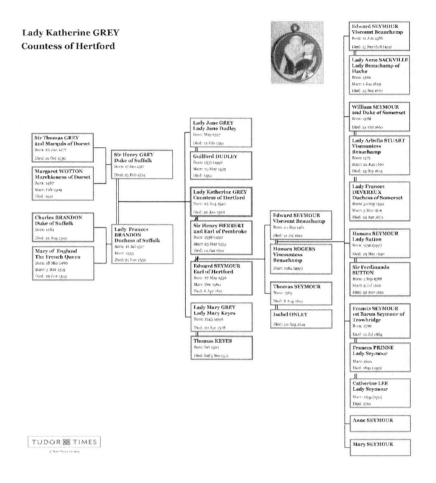

Lady Katherine Grey's Life Story

Chapter 1: Katherine's Family

Lady Katherine Grey was the daughter of Henry Grey, Marquess of Dorset, and his wife, Lady Frances Brandon. Her father was the great-grandson of Queen Elizabeth Woodville, and her mother was even more closely related to Henry VIII, as the daughter of his sister, Mary, the French Queen.

At the time of Katherine's birth, her family were on good terms with their royal cousins. Lady Frances (generally referred to as 'My Lady Marquess') was particularly close to her cousin, Mary, the king's elder daughter. They spent time together and frequently exchanged gifts.

Dorset himself had been favoured by Henry VIII, and, as well as being installed as a Knight of the Bath for the coronation of Anne Boleyn, he was also chosen as the King's Sword Bearer at the actual ceremony. His marriage to the King's niece in 1533, when they were both sixteen, seems to have been as successful as any arranged marriage of the period. The Dorsets had several children, but only three girls, Jane, Katherine herself and Mary, survived infancy.

The young family were brought up largely at Bradgate Park, Leicestershire, and received the best education available. Dorset was strongly inclined to the Reformed faith, and, whether or not his wife totally agreed with him, his daughters were brought up in it. The Grey sisters benefited from the great leap forward in female education that occurred during the last quarter of the fifteenth century, and the first half of the sixteenth. As well as the traditional education of upper class women in household and domestic management, courtly skills such as music, dancing and hunting of various sorts, the girls received an academic education that included Latin and Greek.

The tutor in the Grey household was John Aylmer who had been patronised by Dorset for some years. He later (1577) became Bishop of London, and was a supporter of the legitimacy of female rule (although in a rather half-hearted manner that didn't endear him to Queen Elizabeth). The other men involved in the education of the Grey sisters were their parents' three chaplains – John Haddon, a Fellow of Trinity College, Cambridge; Thomas Harding, holder of the Regius Chair in Hebrew at Oxford, and John Willock, a former Dominican friar. All four of these men who influenced Katherine's education were, at that time, convinced reformers. (Harding later returned to the Catholic fold, and was treated to an excoriating written attack from Jane Grey). All his life Dorset was a keen supporter of scholarship and learning, particularly in the more radical elements of the Reformed faith.

Chapter 2: Royal Succession

When Katherine was seven years old, she came to hold a place in the English succession. The Act of Succession of 1544 named Henry's three children, Edward, Mary and Elizabeth, in that order (ignoring the fact that both daughters had been declared illegitimate). With no further stipulations, the Crown would then have passed from Elizabeth to her heirs under common law – the descendants of her oldest aunt, Margaret, Queen of Scots. However, the 1544 Act had a further provision, permitting Henry VIII to change the succession, should he so wish. Henry took advantage of this latter clause, making a new will not long before his death in January 1547, which had a different effect, putting the line of his younger sister, Mary, the French Queen, directly after

Elizabeth and naming *'the heirs of the body of Lady Frances'* to follow
Elizabeth.

Thus, in January 1547, on the accession of Edward VI, Lady Katherine
Grey became fourth in line to the throne – a great step up from the
position of eighth which she would have held under common law.
Nevertheless, it seems highly unlikely that Katherine would have known
anything about it, or understood it if she had.

As King Edward's reign began, Katherine continued her education,
dividing her time between Bradgate and Dorset House in London. But
intrigue was beginning to surround the family. The Lord Protector,
Edward Seymour, Duke of Somerset, had not chosen to avail himself of
the advice of his younger brother, Sir Thomas Seymour, nor that of
Dorset and this caused resentment. In the later years of Henry's reign,
Dorset had taken rather a back seat. He was not generally popular in
Government circles: he was considered to be *'without sense'* – a
reputation he soon lived up to.

Dorset was also disgruntled at the rash of new titles being handed out.
Ahead of him in rank had been only the Duke of Norfolk, and his wife's
half-brother, the Duke of Suffolk. Now, Edward Seymour had
appropriated a Dukedom, and raised his friend, William Parr, brother of
Queen Katherine, to a Marquessate as well. Thomas Seymour and
Dorset, resentful at being left out of the Privy Council under Henry's will,
began to look for other means of increasing their influence.

Seymour smoothly married his former sweetheart, Katherine Parr, the
Queen Dowager. He also began a flirtation (to put it mildly) with his new
wife's stepdaughter, the Lady Elizabeth. He persuaded Dorset that, if
Dorset's elder daughter, Lady Jane, were committed to his care, he would
be able to arrange a marriage between her and the King. Dorset agreed
to sell Jane's wardship for £2,000. This was by no means an unusual
step – most aristocratic adolescents were sent to live in other households,

although it was less common to transfer the wardship and marriage if the parents were still alive. With Jane's departure, Katherine was now the eldest daughter at home. She began studying Greek under the tutelage of Thomas Harding.

Chapter 3: Unrest

In September 1548, following the death of Katherine Parr in childbed, Jane returned home. Seymour's initial attempts to have her returned to his care, to a household to be presided over by his mother, were rejected by both Dorset and Lady Frances. He persisted, however, and Jane went back to Sudeley. Seymour was becoming more and more reckless in his plotting to obtain power by undermining his brother, Somerset, and Dorset supported him. By March 1549, Seymour had over-reached himself and was executed. Katherine was reunited with her sister again when Seymour's household was broken up.

During the summer of 1548, the rituals of the old religion had been swept away. Use of the rosary was forbidden and a wave of iconoclasm smashed images and stained glass. Prayers for the dead were abandoned, and the chantries, where priests had been paid to pray for souls for all eternity, were closed. For Katherine, brought up in a household that had already eschewed these rituals, little would have changed, but for the vast majority of the population, these changes were not welcome. Katherine, now nine, would probably have been old enough to be aware of the state of the country.

In the west, in the summer of 1549, the Prayer Book rebellion attempted to overturn the new Protestant Communion service. In the east, where Protestantism was more popular, there were uprisings against the enclosure of land – near Bradgate various enclosures had the fences torn down. Matters were compounded by the declaration of war by the French on 17th August, in support of their Scottish allies. The country was in uproar.

Both rebellions were harshly crushed, and, in the fighting, Katherine's uncle, Sir Henry Willoughby, was killed, leaving her cousins as orphans. The oldest, Thomas, came to Bradgate as Dorset's ward and he and his younger siblings, Margaret and Francis, spent a good deal of time with the Grey sisters.

As well as gentry cousins, the Greys had far more impressive relatives, and in November 1549 the Greys travelled to Beaulieu in Essex for a visit to their cousin, the Lady Mary, sister of the King. Lady Mary and Lady Frances had been close friends, although religious differences were beginning to drive a wedge between them. Lady Mary was a staunch conservative, and objected strongly to the religious changes of 1549, whilst the Greys had embraced them – according to Spanish reports, Dorset was 'entirely won over to the new sect.' Nevertheless, Lady Mary showered gifts upon the three girls.

Chapter 4: Ambition

In the aftermath of the summer rebellions, a coup, led by John Dudley, Earl of Warwick overthrew Somerset as Protector. Warwick became Lord President of the Council, and appointed Dorset to a place on it. All of the chief men on the Privy Council were now Protestants (although the term was still not generally used).

Dorset's new position on the Council led to a clutch of honours and offices being granted to him, and the family resided mainly at Dorset House, in London, to give access to the Court.

Based on a passage in one of the Grey tutors, Roger Ascham's, book, *The Schoolmaster*, Dorset and Lady Frances have been characterised as abusive parents, certainly in relation to Katherine's older sister, Jane. Ascham reports that Jane complained, in effect, that nothing she could do pleased her parents, who punished her with nips and pinches.

The biographer of the sisters, Leanda de Lisle, puts this plaint into context, citing more contemporary accounts that suggest that Jane was no more harshly treated than any of her contemporaries, and also pointing out that Jane was a young teenager – an age recognised even in the Tudor period as being one when rebellion against parental authority was normal, although they believed it had to be firmly nipped in the bud.

There are no records of how Katherine felt about the strict regime of study, but she was not destined for greatness like Jane (whom Dorset still fondly believed might one day marry Edward VI) and was not encouraged to be the paragon of learning that her older sister was. Whether this is a reflection of the differing intellectual capacities or tastes between the girls, or the amount of effort expended on Jane, cannot be known. Certainly, Jane was exceptionally intellectually gifted, whilst Katherine seems to have been less interested in academic pursuits.

In 1550, grief struck the family when Lady Frances' two half-brothers, Henry, 2nd Duke of Suffolk, and Charles, died on the same day of the sweating-sickness.

The Duke of Somerset had never been content with having been ousted from the Protectorship and was hoping to be reinstated. Warwick could not stomach the idea, and found means to undermine him, claiming there was a plot by Somerset to capture and murder Warwick and Northampton.

In another round of new honours, orchestrated to strengthen Warwick and his supporters on the Council, the Dukedom of Suffolk was recreated for Dorset and Lady Frances. Warwick was promoted to the Dukedom of Northumberland, and William Herbert, brother-in-law of the late Queen Katherine Parr, and another evangelical, became Earl of

Pembroke. Somerset was arrested, and the new Duke of Suffolk signed the warrant for his removal to the Tower of London, from which he never emerged – Northumberland and Suffolk both sat as judges at his trial.

The Suffolks were riding high and were often at court. On the visit of Marie of Guise, Dowager Queen of Scotland, Frances sat at her left hand at the feast (Lady Mary having declined to attend).

In religious matters, what had begun as evangelicalism and the desire to hear the Word of God, was now moving towards the joylessness that was later associated with Puritanism. In the Suffolk household, the sisters were discouraged from music, and the servants forbidden to play cards. Plainness of dress was also becoming all the rage amongst the 'Godly' in contradistinction to conservatives such as Lady Mary who continued to dress resplendently. Ascham reported that the precocious Lady Jane, on receiving a magnificent dress from Lady Mary, refused it with an insolent message – a step much admired by the evangelicals.

In 1551, a new Prayer Book was prepared. It was far more evangelical in tone than that of 1549, and the Archbishop of Canterbury, Thomas Cranmer, was not entirely happy with some of the more radical proposals – for example, he insisted on the retention of kneeling to receive Communion. For the Greys however, it was very welcome.

Chapter 5: The King's 'Devise for the Succession'

Northumberland's influence over the young king grew. He even persuaded the King to over-rule the Earl of Cumberland's refusal to permit the marriage of his daughter, Margaret Clifford (Frances' niece) to his own fourth son, Lord Guilford Dudley. This marriage, was not, however, to take place. Instead, Northumberland looked to move his family a step closer to the throne with the marriage of Guilford to Katherine's sister Jane (third in line). Edward VI was ill, and the Lady

Mary was reminding the Privy Council of her position as heir. She rode to London in February with a huge retinue, and the Duchesses of Northumberland and Suffolk joined her train as she visited her brother.

Although Edward opened Parliament on 1st March 1553, no substantive business was done, and he was not formerly announced as of age. Soon after, he made a will, called his *'Devise for the Succession'*. Edward was fourteen, exceptionally well-educated and intelligent. The influence of Northumberland and his radical tutors had given him a deep commitment to the Reformed Faith, and his great fear was that the Lady Mary would undo all his good work. Besides, the idea of female rulers was even more unpopular with the Reformers than it had been with Catholics. Bible study had dwelt a good deal on the wickedness of women and their duty of obedience. A particular scourge of womankind was John Knox, later to write his *'First Blast of the Trumpet against the Monstrous Regiment of Women'* and Knox was a chaplain at Edward's court.

The King's Devise named as his heir, the heirs male (not yet born), first of Frances, then of her three daughters, then of her niece, Margaret Clifford, daughter of Eleanor Brandon. In the event of a minority, the boy's mother was permitted to be Regent, provided she did everything her male Councillors advised. If no males had been born by the time of the King's death, Frances was to be Regent – Suffolk must have danced with glee.

For the Privy Councillors, this meant that there were four young women available to be snatched up as matrimonial prizes, by whom they could, potentially, make their sons King. Lady Mary Grey and Lady Margaret Clifford were too young (both only 8 years old), so this left the two older Grey girls.

In early 1553, Katherine and Jane were married in a triple arrangement. Katherine was married to Henry Herbert, the son of

William Herbert, Earl of Pembroke, nephew of the late Katherine Parr; Jane was married to Northumberland's fourth, but oldest unmarried son, Guilford, and Katherine Dudley, Northumberland's daughter, was married to Henry Hastings, who was a great-grandson of Margaret Plantagenet, Countess of Salisbury, and thus carried royal York blood. Ominously, the King was too ill to attend any of the ceremonies, contenting himself with sending presents of *'rich ornaments and jewels'*

The ceremony between Katherine and Herbert took place on 25th May 1553 at the Northumberland residence, Durham House. It was a day of traditional celebrations – feasting, jousting and masquing. Whether Northumberland engineered the marriage of Katherine as part of a wider plot to secure the succession to Jane and his son, is a matter of debate amongst historians.

As more emphasis is placed on Edward's own responsibility for the *'Devise'* so less is placed on Northumberland. Professor Ives, in particular, believes the marriage of Katherine and Herbert was a routine aristocratic arrangement, and that, far from Pembroke being his crony, the two men did not get on well. The counter-argument might be that Pembroke was given the second prize of Katherine, in order to gain his support for the marriage of Jane to Northumberland's son. Support for this may be found in the correspondence of the Imperial Ambassador, who claimed that the marriage was made for Katherine at Northumberland's *'intercession.'*

Katherine was twelve, which was the age of consent for marriage, but generally considered to be too young for consummation. Nevertheless, she went to live at the Pembroke home at their London property, Baynard's Castle, together with her fifteen year old husband. He had been in poor health at the time of their wedding, but soon made a recovery and the young couple grew fond of each other.

Meanwhile, Edward, close to death, had made another change to his *Devise*. It was apparent that no boys would be born before he died, so he bequeathed the throne, not to Frances, but to Lady Jane and her heirs male. As Jane was now firmly under the thumb of Northumberland (or so the Duke thought) Northumberland could picture a world in which his pre-eminence continued for some time.

Chapter 6: The Queen's Sister

On 6th July 1553, Edward died, and the following day the Mayor and City dignitaries swore oaths of allegiance to Queen Jane. Katherine was still living at Baynard's Castle with her husband and father-in-law, Pembroke. She could look forward to a glorious future as sister to the Queen and Countess of Pembroke with a husband she was growing to love – for a Tudor noblewomen, life could hardly promise to be more enjoyable.

By 19th July, however, the Lady Mary had triumphantly overturned the coup. On that day, Pembroke, convened a meeting of Councillors and the Lord Mayor at Baynard's Castle and they agreed that they would process to Cheapside to proclaim Mary as queen.

When the news arrived at the Tower, Suffolk was persuaded to proclaim Mary Queen from Tower Hill, and then inform Jane that her reign was over. Suffolk and Frances then left Jane to her fate with the Dudleys and went to Baynard's Castle.

Before long, Suffolk was under arrest in the Tower, but Frances had raced to intercept Mary at Beaulieu, and beg her forgiveness, placing as much blame as she could on Northumberland, and pleading that Suffolk had been coerced and poisoned by the Duke.

Mary, who was of a forgiving nature (leaving religion aside) promptly issued pardons for Frances and Suffolk, and was only dissuaded from doing the same for Jane by the urgings of the Imperial Ambassador.

Katherine was now placed in a very unhappy position as Pembroke, who had also been pardoned, sought to distance himself from the debacle of the coup. He wanted the marriage between Katherine and his son annulled. The young couple, who had become attached to each other, swore that despite her youth (she was still not quite thirteen years old) they had consummated the marriage. Even if that were true, which is unlikely, no-one was prepared to listen to them and she was packed off back to her mother.

Had Suffolk been prepared to pay even lip-service to Mary's re-introduction of the old faith, and accept her decision to marry Prince Philip of Spain, it is likely that both he and Jane would have had their lives spared. Instead, he first stirred up trouble in religious matters, and, according to the Imperial Ambassador, this annoyed the Queen

'The Duke of Suffolk is doing bad work in connection with religion, and the Queen is angry with him for his manner of abusing her clemency and good nature'

He then became involved in outright rebellion, taking part in what is known as Wyatt's Rebellion, an uprising that sought to overthrow Mary and replace her with Elizabeth, who was of a more Protestant bent, although nowhere near so radical or idealistic as Jane Grey. The revolt was a complete failure, and, whether the intention was to replace Mary with Elizabeth, or with Jane, the result was the same. Death warrants for Jane, her husband Guilford, and Suffolk were signed.

Mary still hoped to save her young cousin, both body and soul, and delayed the execution in the hope that Jane could be converted to the Catholic faith, sending a priest of her own, Dr Feckenham, to try to persuade her. Jane was steadfast in her religion, and glorying in martyrdom as only a sixteen year old idealist can, accepted her fate. One of her last actions was a gift to Katherine, of her Greek New Testament, with a message written on the blank leaves. The letter is strongly evangelical in tone, exhorting Katherine to put away the things of the world and be prepared for death at any time:

'I have here sent you, my dear sister Katherine, a book, which although it be not outwardly trimmed with gold...yet inwardly it is of more worth than all the precious mines that the vast earth can boast of. It is the book, my only best and best-loved sister, of the Law of the Lord. It is the Testament and last will...which shall lead you to the path of eternal joy and if you with a good mind read it, and with an earnest mind do purpose to follow it, it shall bring you to an immortal and everlasting life..... It shall teach you to live, and shall learn you to die...My good sister, once more again let me entreat you to learn to die; deny the world, defy the devil, and despise the flesh, and delight yourself only in the Lord. Be penitent for your sins, and yet despair not; be strong in faith, yet presume not; and desire with St Paul to be dissolved and to be with Christ, with whom, even in death, there is life...Now as touching my death, rejoice as I do, my dearest sister, that I shall be delivered of this corruption, and put on incorruption: for I am assured that I shall, for losing of a mortal life, win one that is immortal, joyful and everlasting....I pray...(that you may) die in the true Christian faith, from the which (in God's name) I exhort that you never swerve, neither for hope of life nor for fear of death...Fare you well, good sister, and put your only trust in God, who only must help you.'

Jane and Guilford died on 12th February 1554 and within two weeks Katherine also lost her father to the axe. He, too, was steadfast in his evangelical faith

Frances was now left to salvage what she could from the ruin of her husband's mixture of ambition, religious zealotry, and lack of political skill. The Suffolk estates were forfeit to the Crown, but within a couple of months Queen Mary had re-granted various of the family's possessions.

Chapter 109: The Queen's Cousin

By July 1554, France, Katherine and her younger sister, Mary, were at court, granted positions of honour in the Queen's Privy Chamber. That month was a busy one for Queen Mary and her ladies. On 25th she was married at Winchester Cathedral to Philip of Spain. Katherine and her former husband were both present at the celebrations, Katherine in a new red velvet gown provided by the Queen. On their return to London, Mary and Philip, with the rest of their train, spent the night at Suffolk House before entering the capital. One wonders how Katherine viewed her old home, now housing Mary and Philip as sovereigns, rather than Jane and Guilford.

Katherine was making friends amongst her fellow courtiers, including Elizabeth (Bess) Hardwick, wife of Sir William Cavendish. Katherine was godmother to their first child, and using her privilege of choosing the name, selected Elizabeth. This has been read as a signal that Katherine was showing support for her cousin Elizabeth, and the Protestant faction, but, since Katherine was only fourteen, and at no time displayed either religious zealotry or any political cunning whatsoever, it is probably safer to assume that she just named the baby after the mother.

Katherine's best friend, however, was Lady Jane Seymour, daughter of the Duke of Somerset, and his second wife, Anne Stanhope. Named for her aunt, Queen Jane, the young Jane Seymour had been brought up to be nearly as intellectually precocious as Katherine's sister and a strong adherent of the Reformed faith. She too, had once been considered as a possible bride for her cousin, Edward VI. Now, the girls idled away their hours in the time-honoured pursuits of young women – chatting, and sharing confidences about the young men they fancied. Katherine, unhappy at the dissolution of her marriage to Herbert, still hoped that they would be reunited.

Herbert was also making his way at court, and in 1557 would be amongst the young men who went to France in the army led by King Philip against Henri II. At first victorious in the Battle of St Quentin, Philip's accustomed hesitancy meant that he failed to follow up the victory in a march to Paris. Henri II, desperate for revenge, retaliated by an onslaught on the poorly provisioned and defended town of Calais, which fell in January 1558 – the last remnant of Henry II's empire that had stretched from Hadrian's Wall to the Pyrenees.

The loss of Calais infected the Queen and the court with depression, at the beginning of a terrible year for the whole country – poor harvests, worse weather, and a virulent strain of influenza scourged the country. Lady Jane Seymour fell ill, and returned to her mother at Hanworth House for nursing. Katherine went with her and spent the summer of 1558 in a combination of care for her friend, and young love.

For Lady Jane's brother, another Edward Seymour, was also at Hanworth. Seymour was a year or so older than Katherine. The young couple fell in love, and aided by Lady Jane, passed messages and notes between each other. He even asked his sister to find out whether Katherine would marry him.

At this point, scenting danger, Seymour's mother intervened, no doubt pointing out to the young man that to marry a woman of royal blood, without the Queen's express permission, was an act likely to end in the shedding of tears, if not the shedding of blood.

Seymour, in the time-honoured fashion of adolescents, shook off his mother's advice, and maintained that there was nothing wrong with

Katherine and he being together, either at home or at Court, unless the Queen forbade it.

At the end of the summer, Katherine and Jane Seymour returned to Court. Jane was better, but this illness may have weakened her lungs. The Queen however, was now seriously ill. She too, had caught the influenza, and was still suffering from whatever disease (possibly ovarian cancer) had falsely led her to believe herself pregnant. By mid-November, forty-two year old Mary was dead. Katherine, as one of her ladies, would have been involved in the preparations for the funeral. Her feelings for the queen as she watched over the body during the month-long lying in state are likely to have been mixed. Mary was responsible for the death of Katherine's father and sister (no matter how much they may have deserved it by the standards of the time) yet she had been forgiving and generous to Frances and Katherine herself.

But there were not just her personal feelings of either grief or rejoicing. Katherine was now heir to the throne under the terms of Henry VIII's will.

Chapter 7: The Queen's Heir

In later years, when quizzed on Mary, Queen of Scots, another possible successor, Elizabeth asked drily '..*think you.. that I could love my own winding sheet?*' and that dislike of her possible heirs manifested itself within days of her accession. Katherine was demoted from Queen Mary's Privy Chamber, the inner sanctum of the court, to the Presence Chamber, a place to which any member of the nobility or higher ranks of the gentry had access. She had a part, with other ladies of the court, in the coronation procession through London, but no special treatment.

On the bright side, her lover had had his father's earlier title of Earl of Hertford resurrected and bestowed on him in a new creation. The Duchy of Somerset, however, was not re-granted. It can probably be inferred from this, that no rumour of an attachment between Katherine and Hertford the preceding summer had reached Elizabeth. She certainly wouldn't have wished to promote a young man who had been sniffing around an heir to the throne.

There was immediate pressure on the new Queen to marry, but Elizabeth prevaricated. With hindsight, her choice not to marry looks like a brilliant decision, but we cannot infer that Elizabeth ever made that deliberate choice – at least, not in the early years of her reign. Mediaeval and Tudor minds just did not consider a state of non-marriage as a possible choice (with the exception in earlier times of entering a religious order). At the lowest levels of society, marriage was more or less an economic necessity, as neither men nor women could function alone as an effective economic unit. Higher up the social scale, it was a duty to marry to beget heirs, and at the top of the hierarchy, it was a self-evident truth that a monarch should beget a legitimate heir as soon as possible.

Elizabeth's hesitations were around when she ought to marry and to whom, given that both a home-grown consort, and a foreign prince had draw-backs. So long as she did remain unmarried, however, her heir was likely to be courted, as she had been during Mary's reign. It was thus prudent to treat any pretensions to being her successor that Katherine might have, coldly.

Katherine was well aware of the meaning of her demotion, complaining to Count Feria, the Spanish Ambassador that:

'the Queen [did] not wish her to succeed in case of her (Elizabeth's) death without heirs.'

Feria, who knew Katherine well, as he was to marry Jane Dormer, one of Katherine's former colleagues as maid-of-honour to Queen Mary, described her as *'dissatisfied'* and *'offended'* at Elizabeth's treatment of her. It was also reported that she had spoken disrespectfully to the Queen.

Chapter 8: Politics

Wider European politics now came into play. With Mary's death, England's alignment with Hapsburg Spain and Empire was weakened, but the French (who previously had intrigued to overthrow Mary in the Wyatt Rebellion with the ostensible goal of putting Elizabeth on the throne) were now promoting the claims of Mary, Queen of Scots. The Hapsburg interest would be best served by a marriage between Elizabeth, and her former brother-in-law, Philip II, or with one of his Imperial cousins. If that could not be achieved, then the Hapsburgs needed a viable alternative to Mary, Queen of Scots to support. Katherine Grey might be the very one!

Feria courted Katherine's support. He suggested that a Spanish or Imperial husband might suit her, and she agreed that she would not marry without his agreement, nor change her religion – Katherine had conformed to the reintroduced Catholic practices of Mary's reign. There were rumours that Feria even went so far as to arrange an abduction of Katherine with a view to smuggling her to Spain. From the extant records, it is impossible to tell whether Katherine was privy to this plan. It was abandoned when Henri II of France died, the Spanish believing that his heir, the young François II, was much less likely to consider invasions of England – he was too young and untried to begin his reign with extravagant military ventures, even in favour of his young wife, the Queen of Scots.

Katherine's statement that she would not change her religion without consulting Feria (if his remarks are to be believed) is unlikely to have been a genuine declaration of Katherine's religious views. So far as is recorded, she complied with the Act of Uniformity, and all of the support for her position as heir was grounded on the belief that she was a Protestant. Katherine may have made this comment to leave open the idea of a Spanish match. She probably warmed to the idea, as during the summer of 1559, Hertford seemed to have lost interest in her.

He initially excused himself from attending the Queen's progress that set out from London on 17th July 1559. They met again, however, at Eltham, and were soon deeply in love. It was an enchanted summer for the young couple – masques, banquets, hunting parties and dancing filled the days and the fragrant summer evenings at Eltham and Nonsuch. Hertford's intentions were strictly honourable, and later in the year, probably in September or October, he formally requested Lady Frances to sanction his marriage to her daughter.

Lady Frances and her second husband, Adrian Stokes, were pleased with the plans, but they were well aware that the Queen might not approve. Their advice to Hertford was to persuade as many of Elizabeth's advisors and Privy Councillors as possible of the benefits of the match. A letter was drafted for Frances to send to the Queen, once there was sufficient support for the match, asking the Queen's consent. Frances also confirmed with Katherine that she wished the marriage to take place – the fashion for arranging marriages for young people without consulting them was beginning to fade.

Hertford's initial feelers to Privy Councillors met with the advice that he should not attempt to rush matters. Whilst Katherine was waiting to formalise the betrothal, her mother, who had been ailing for several years, died. The funeral, paid for by Elizabeth, in an unusual access of generosity, took place in Westminster Abbey. Katherine, her eldest surviving child, was chief mourner, following the coffin. The funeral was conducted according to the rites and ceremonies laid down in Elizabeth's

Act of Uniformity, which, although Protestant, was not as radical as the faith that had been espoused by Frances' husband and Jane.

Chapter 9: The Queen's Rival

Katherine was now in a sort of limbo – in mourning for her mother, not yet betrothed although she was nearly twenty, by which time most girls of her class were married, and with no formal role at Court. She was still, however, being courted by the Spanish, who were gleeful at the prospect that Elizabeth's open infatuation with Lord Robert Dudley was causing murmurs of disquiet. If she were overthrown in favour of an heir over whom they had more influence than on the steely Elizabeth, England might be brought back into the Hapsburg sphere.

In early 1560, rumours had reached the France and the Low Countries about Spanish plans. One of Cecil's informants, John Middleton wrote:

'I am told that there is practising for a marriage to be made betwixt the Prince of Spain and the Lady Katherine Grey, which is not of the best liked for divers respects, and by some hindered.'

Elizabeth, who was having probably the most enjoyable six months of her life pursuing a passionate, if platonic, relationship with Dudley, was not blind to the overtures being made to Katherine by Spain. She decided to out-charm the Spanish Ambassador by suddenly taking Katherine by the hand, restoring her to the Privy Chamber and keeping her at her side – even saying she might adopt her cousin – a scheme as far-fetched as may be imagined!

Meanwhile, Hertford's sister, Lady Jane, and their brother, Henry, were promoting the marriage – passing billets-doux between the young lovers and facilitating secret meetings. It is clear that at these meetings, nothing more intimate than hand-holding took place.

As another attempt to downplay Katherine's importance, Sir William Cecil, Elizabeth's chief minister, told the Spanish Ambassador that, in the event of Elizabeth's untimely demise, a third queen-regnant in a row would be quite unacceptable, and that Henry Hastings, Earl of Huntingdon and great-grandson of Margaret Plantagenet, Countess of Salisbury, would be preferred.

Huntingdon was a committed Protestant. Known as '*the Puritan Earl*', he was a brother-in-law of Lord Robert Dudley. It is evident, nevertheless, that Cecil, although he would prefer Elizabeth to marry suitably and beget children, favoured Katherine as her heir. There was talk of marrying her to the son of the Earl of Arran, who was Mary, Queen of Scots' nearest male heir, although he was also a suitor for the Queen.

Scandal regarding Elizabeth and Dudley reached epic proportions when his wife, Amy Robsart, was found dead in mysterious circumstances. Had the Queen then married him, she would surely have lost her throne, if not her life. Elizabeth might have loved Dudley, but she loved her crown, her honour and her country more. She soon made it clear that there would be no marriage.

In the light of this cooling of the Queen's relationship with her favourite, her marriage to a suitable European prince once again moved to the top of the her Council's agenda. Cecil took the opportunity to warn Hertford that he should back off from plans to marry Katherine.

Chapter 113: Secret Marriage

It is difficult to imagine that Katherine, who had borne the loss of her sister for attempting to interfere with the succession, can really have been so naïve as to believe that Elizabeth would easily forgive a marriage that was not sanctioned by her, especially as Katherine had shown herself disgruntled when the Queen had not acknowledged her openly as her heir.

Perhaps she believed that marriage to a known Protestant of good standing would actually enhance her position – certainly those nobles in favour of a Protestant succession would welcome a married woman with a son rather than another childless queen. Perhaps Katherine thought that Cecil's tacit support would be enough to extricate her from any problems. Perhaps, though, it was just love.

Hertford took Cecil's warning seriously and backed off – even flirting with another lady. Katherine was distraught and wrote to him. Unable to distance himself from her, Hertford wrote a reassuring letter, suggesting a secret betrothal, to which Katherine agreed. Betrothal was as binding as marriage and could only be set aside with the Church's permission. Hertford and Katherine exchanged promises with his sister, Jane, as witness. Katherine received a diamond betrothal ring, and Hertford commissioned a gold wedding ring, inscribed with verses of his own invention.

Whilst betrothal was binding, it could be dissolved with Church sanction. For marriage, consummation must take place, and Katherine and Hertford were no doubt eager to fulfil the requirements.

The next time the Queen left Court, for a hunting trip, Katherine cried off, claiming she had the tooth-ache. She and Jane were allowed to stay behind. The next day, they left Whitehall and went to Hertford's house at Cannon Row. Hertford later testified that the date had not been pre-arranged, that they had just agreed that Katherine would come as soon as she could. Hertford sent most of his servants away, although some of the kitchen staff remained, and they later testified to Katherine having come to the house on that day.

Whilst Hertford and Katherine greeted each other, Jane slipped out to find a priest, although whether she just picked the first one she saw, or whether the groom had previously engaged him is unclear. The wedding service, according to the authorised Book of Common Prayer, was completed, and Jane left the couple together.

The marriage thoroughly consummated, Katherine and Jane returned to Whitehall. Over the next few months, Katherine and her new husband took every opportunity they could to be together. It was pretty much an open secret, at least amongst their servants and immediate friends, that they were sleeping together, even if no-one knew about their marital status. Katherine was taxed on the matter by Elizabeth's friend, Geraldine, Lady Clinton, but denied that she was *'familiar'* with the earl.

In early 1561, Cecil, still concerned that Hertford was paying too much attention to Katherine, suggested that he might like to travel abroad. A suggestion from Cecil was as good as a command, but Hertford, although he was probably thrilled at the idea of seeing France and Italy at Crown expense, hesitated. His mother wrote to Cecil that she was happy for Edward to go abroad, and that Cecil was to overrule his wilfulness. The Duchess mentioned that she would like him to be *'matched to some noble house to the Queen's liking'*. With pressure from the Duchess and Cecil, Hertford agreed. He told Jane that he would go, and she broke the news to Katherine.

Katherine thought that she might be pregnant. If she were, according to Hertford, there could be no solution but to tell the Queen of their marriage and hope she would be forgiving. Katherine hesitated. Perhaps she wasn't pregnant after all. Soon, her own health was the least of her preoccupations. Her friend, and now sister-in-law, Jane, was mortally ill, and died on 29th March 1561. She was buried in Westminster Abbey, next to Katherine's mother.

Both Katherine and Hertford grieved for Jane, and this may have affected Katherine's health. She could not tell Hertford for certain whether she was pregnant. He told her that he would not leave for

Europe if she were, but if not, he would go. Nevertheless, he would 'not tarry long' if it transpired she was going to have a baby.

Before his departure, Hertford drew up a will, granting Katherine lands to the value of £1,000 per annum, which he gave to her, together with some ready cash, and then departed for Europe. Cecil took the opportunity to warn Katherine again about the risks of consorting with the Earl without royal approval.

It was far too late for Katherine to draw back now. She was certainly about to bear a child, and the Queen, after the short period of favour, had once again turned hostile. Only twenty, with her husband abroad and not answering the letters she sent, her parents and older sister dead, and her best friend and sister-in-law also gone, Katherine panicked. She cast about for another solution, and remembered her first husband, Henry Herbert. If she had actually been validly married to him back in 1553, Elizabeth could not reasonably be angry with her for that, and any affair she might have had with Hertford would not have the taint of treason.

She wrote to Herbert, saying she believed they were still married. At the time of the annulment, they had pleaded to stay together, so perhaps she believed he would be fond enough of her to accept paternity of her child. Herbert began to court her, sending pictures and gifts, whilst Katherine still sought to contact Hertford. On discovering this, Herbert withdrew his attentions and sent her a stinging letter, accusing her of 'whoredom' and attempting to 'entrap' him with sugared bait. He demanded the return of the letters he had sent her. Katherine did not immediately comply, leading him to write a further letter, threatening her with exposure if she did not send his notes back.

Chapter 10: The Queen's Prisoner

That summer, the Court progressed through the eastern counties, arriving in Ipswich on 5th August 1561. The same night, Katherine confessed her pregnancy to a lady by the name of St Loe. The identity of this lady is disputed. Biographers of Bess of Hardwick usually assume it to be her. This would seem a perfectly reasonable proposition – as noted earlier, Katherine was the godmother of Bess' daughter by her second marriage to William Cavendish. Katherine's biographer, Leanda de Lisle, however identifies St Loe (or Sentlow) as Bess' sister-in-law. Whoever the recipient of Katherine's confidences was, she was refused to get involved.

The next day, Katherine sought out Lord Robert Dudley, and confessed all. Lord Robert agreed to be *'a means to the Queen's Highness'* and told Elizabeth the whole tale. Elizabeth was incandescent – as she would always be when secret marriages were revealed. Whilst the main thrust of her anger was in Katherine's threat to the succession, any hint of immoral behaviour at her court reflected badly on her, and gave fodder to the gossips who speculated about her behaviour with Dudley.

Katherine was immediately arrested and sent to the Tower, and Hertford recalled from Europe.

Orders were given to Sir Edward Warner, the Lieutenant of the Tower, to question Katherine strictly. Warner had been Lieutenant during the brief reign of Lady Jane Grey, and he must have regretted seeing her sister brought to the Tower. He was also detailed to find out who had known about the secret match and to tell Katherine that her only hope for mercy was to tell the complete truth.

Hertford, who had returned as commanded, was arrested when he docked at Dover, and despatched to the Tower as well.

Over the succeeding weeks, the couple were interrogated numerous times by the Privy Council, as was Katherine's step-father, Adrian Stokes, who had been involved in the early discussions between Hertford and Frances about a possible marriage. Their accounts of their courtship, betrothal and marriage did not tally entirely, particularly in that Hertford did not recollect Frances ever having drafted a letter to the Queen – although, of course, he may not have known of it. Hertford's mother, Anne, Duchess of Somerset distanced herself from her 'unruly child' with a letter to the Queen protesting her own loyalty.

The couple remained in the Tower, forbidden to have contact. Katherine delivered a son on 21st September 1561. He was christened Edward, for his father and grandfather, and a couple of the Tower officials served as his god-parents. Elizabeth, further enraged by the birth of a son to her potential heir, kept the couple in prison.

Whilst this seems harsh, they had, in fact broken the law – a Statute of 1536 had forbidden the marriage of a member of the royal family without the sovereign's permission. Elizabeth was making quite clear that her personal preference for the succession was the traditional route of primogeniture, which would put Mary, Queen of Scots' claim first, but she would not make any official declarations on the topic. Elizabeth also believed that there was more to the matter between Katherine and Hertford than love-sick youth, hinting that some of her Councillors were behind the match.

In the outside world, Cecil and Elizabeth's other councillors were pushing for settlement of the succession by a Parliamentary act. For Elizabeth this was anathema – to suggest that the succession be laid down by Parliament was to suggest that the sovereign answered to Parliament, rather than the reverse. For this reason, if no other, she would always prefer the claim of the Queen of Scots – above all, monarchs should stand together to enforce their rights.

With this level of pressure on her, Elizabeth was determined to undermine Katherine's claim – showing her as the mother of a bastard child would certainly not do her credibility any good. On 31st January, 1562, an ecclesiastical commission was set up, under Matthew Parker, Archbishop of Canterbury, and the details of the couple's union examined.

What constituted marriage was not absolutely clear-cut. Prior to the Reformation, the general view was that consent, a statement that the couple were marrying or planning to marry, plus consummation was sufficient, provided both parties either agreed they had consented, or there were witnesses to the promise. The Book of Common Prayer adopted in 1559 required banns to have been read on at least three Sundays, or a licence to have been given by the Archbishop to obviate the need for banns, but this irregularity did not necessarily invalidate the match.

In this case, much was made of the fact that no witnesses could be produced – Jane Seymour was dead, and the couple had not bothered to find out the name or address of the priest who had officiated. If any official efforts were made to track him down, they failed, either for lack of rigour or because he preferred to avoid the role of scapegoat. The Commission, therefore, in a decision that can hardly have come as a surprise to anyone, in view of the Queen's attitude, declared the marriage invalid on 12th May 1562, and the baby Edward as illegitimate.

Chapter 11: Punishment

Despite the judgement, Katherine and Hertford themselves stuck to their belief in the validity of their marriage. Still languishing in the Tower (although in all the comfort appropriate to her status, with her pets) Katherine clearly inspired sympathy for her plight. On at least two occasions, the gaolers turned a blind eye to a couple of unlocked doors that led to meetings. These meetings led to Katherine falling pregnant again. It would be difficult for the illegitimacy of this child to be impugned, as both parents had stated their belief in their marriage in front of no less a witness than the Archbishop of Canterbury himself!

In the summer of 1562, the succession question became urgent as Elizabeth fell ill with small-pox. Katherine's claims were pressed by some of the Council, but others preferred Mary, Queen of Scots, the Earl of Huntingdon, or the Countess of Lennox (who in strict primogeniture would follow Mary of Scotland and had the advantage of being born in England). Elizabeth recovered, but the new Parliament (carefully managed to ensure a Protestant majority) pushed her to name a successor.

Elizabeth refused. She assured the Commons that she had every intention of marrying and begetting an heir – she just wasn't able to say exactly when. Into this tense situation, Katherine's pregnancy was announced. The scale of Elizabeth's fury was beyond measure. The Lieutenant of the Tower was to be imprisoned for enabling the meetings to take place, and on the day the child (another boy, named Thomas) was christened in February 1563, Hertford was brought before the Star Chamber for further interrogation. The story of how he had bribed the warders was revealed, together with details of his visits to Katherine.

Hertford was found guilty on three counts – deflowering a royal virgin, breaking out of his prison, and repeating his criminal behaviour. He was fined £15,000 in total and ordered back to the Tower to remain there at the Queen's pleasure.

Katherine and Hertford both remained in the Tower, and now there was no hope of meeting. Hertford wrote importunate letters to Dudley, asking him to intercede with the Queen, even sending her a pair of gloves as a sweetener, but to no avail.

Katherine's relatives also pleaded on her behalf. In March 1563, Lord John Grey, her uncle, wrote a strongly worded letter to Cecil, expatiating on Katherine's misery and condemning the Queen's hard-heartedness:

'In faithe, I wolde I were the Queene's Confessor this Lent, that I might joine her in penaunce to forgeve and forget; or otherwise able to steppe into the pulpett, to tell her Highnes, that God will not forgeve her, unleast she felye forgeve all the worlde...'

It is unlikely that Cecil shared these sentiments with the Queen!

Chapter 12: House Arrest

The summer of 1563 saw an outbreak of plague. By August, the number of deaths had increased to such a level that Elizabeth was begged to send Katherine, her children and Hertford out of London for their own safety. She agreed, and Katherine, together with her younger son, was released to the custody of her uncle, Lord John Grey, at Pirgo in Essex. Lord John was warned Katherine was only being released from the Tower for fear of illness, not to be free.

Hertford was permitted to live with his mother at Hanworth House. Katherine's oldest son went with his father, to be brought up by Anne, Duchess of Somerset.

Once Katherine had arrived at his home, Grey wrote again to Cecil, assuring him of Katherine's penitence. In a rather ironic testament, both to Elizabeth's fears in regard to naming a successor, and her parsimony, Hertford was obliged to defray the costs of Katherine's household, despite the validity of their marriage being denied. Her household consisted of three ladies, three man-servants, a 'lackey', a nurse for the baby, and a two women to wash both her's and the baby's linen.

In addition she had a quantity of furniture, including five pieces of tapestry, a *'changeable'* (presumably what we would call *'shot'*) silk damask bedspread, a red and gold-striped silk quilt, numerous pillows of different levels of softness, footstools and cupboards. Whilst this sounds rather grand, apparently the furniture was largely worn out and shabby. It had also been damaged by Katherine's own monkeys and dogs during her time in the Tower.

In November, Katherine wrote a humble letter to the Queen, begging her pardon and mercy. It was forwarded by Grey to Cecil, with a view to having it first approved and then forwarded by Robert Dudley – this would be Katherine's best hope of forgiveness.

Elizabeth remained adamantine in the face of Katherine's pleading. Katherine then seems to have fallen into depression. Lord John informed Cecil in December 1563, that she was constantly weeping, would not leave her room, and was not eating properly.

Katherine wrote yet another humble letter to Cecil, but, perhaps rather tactlessly, signed it *'Katheryne Hartford'*. She also wrote to her husband, in a letter recently brought back into the light by her biographer, Leanda de Lisle, it having lain hidden after its original Victorian compiler declined to publish its unusually explicit content. Katherine wrote that she

> *'long[s] to be merry with [him] as when [their] little sweet boy in the Tower was gotten...'*

Chapter 13: The Succession Question

Katherine was a figure of sympathy for many – why should she not marry at her pleasure? But others considered the behaviour of the young couple as foolish at best, and treasonable at worst. Whilst the country outside London was still, in the early 1560s, traditional in religious practice, London was at the forefront of Protestant thought. Katherine's sister, Lady Jane Grey, was considered a Protestant martyr, and there were several publications, including John Foxe's *'Book of Acts and Monuments'* (Foxe's Book of Martyrs) that capitalised on the Grey adherence to the new faith. Katherine, now with two sons, was their prime candidate for the succession.

Her claims were tabulated in a book by the MP John Hales, possibly aided by Cecil (certainly Lord Robert thought so, and Nicholas Bacon, Keeper of the Great Seal, agreed). Hales, who was the Member of Parliament for Lancaster, had been a member of Edward VI's Government, and was an associate of the more Protestant leaning of Elizabeth's ministers. He not only espoused Katherine as heir, but also declared that her marriage was legal, despite the findings of the Archbishop's Court. Not content with writing his book, he brought the matter up in the House of Commons – this led to a speedy dispatch to the Fleet prison, followed by a sojourn in the Tower, and then house arrest for almost the rest of his life. Such was the danger of meddling with the succession, and Katherine and Hertford too, continued to face the consequences.

Whatever Elizabeth might have wanted to do (and there is no evidence that she had anything but dislike for her Grey cousins), to free Katherine would have undermined her strategy to keep the succession in abeyance, or if she couldn't avoid specifying an heir, settle it on Mary, Queen of Scots, whom she hoped to neutralise by arranging a marriage for her with her own favourite, Robert Dudley. Hertford was returned to the Tower on 26th May 1564, and Katherine moved to even stricter supervision under Sir William Petre at Ingatestone Hall. Her uncle was too partisan, and was sent to the Tower himself to contemplate the Queen's displeasure.

More pleas were made – from the Duchess of Somerset to Cecil, and Hertford to Dudley, who counselled patience. Sometime during the summer, Hertford was released to the custody of Sir John Mason, who heartily disliked him, while Katherine remained at Ingatestone.

Despite her imprisonment, she was still seen as a potential heir to the throne. In 1565, Philip of Spain thought it possible that she would be named as successor as an act of revenge by Elizabeth and the English Parliament following the marriage of Mary, Queen of Scots to Lord Darnley, who was the nearest male heir to Elizabeth. However, it did not happen.

Chapter 14: The End

Katherine was to stay at Ingatestone for two years, before being moved in May 1566 to the home of Sir John Wentworth at Gosfield Hall, a distant cousin of Hertford's. Sir John was not happy at the arrival of such a troublesome prisoner. Well into his seventies, he declared that he would rather be imprisoned himself than be custodian of Katherine. He pointed out how easy it would be for her to escape. Katherine did not attempt to escape, but she and Hertford still corresponded.

During 1566, calls for the succession to be assured were again brought forward by Parliament, with Katherine still favoured by the majority of the Protestant faction - although not all. Dudley was inclined to support the claims of Mary, Queen of Scots, who now had a son. Elizabeth, with her usual skill, managed to evade the issue yet again.

Then came the bombshell that overshadowed politics in England and Scotland for the next twenty-five years. The Queen of Scots' husband, Lord Darnley, had been murdered, and Mary deposed, accused of complicity in his death. Yet another wave of uncertainty over the succession washed over Elizabeth and her ministers, with the rival factions supporting Katherine and Mary each pushing their own candidate forward. Meanwhile, Katherine herself was still isolated in Essex, although she was now permitted to enjoy the rents of some of the lands previously owned by her parents.

By the end of 1567, poor Sir John Wentworth had died, and his widow and executor were at their wits' end with no orders as to what to do with their young prisoner. She was moved to even stricter confinement at Cockfield Hall in Suffolk, under the wardenship of a protesting Sir Owen Hopton.

As soon as he saw her, Hopton realised that Katherine was ill. He requested that the Queen's own doctor, Dr Symonds, be sent to treat her. Katherine however, did not want to get better. She lay in bed, depressed, not eating and with no hopes for the future. She listened to the psalms being read to her and although the Hoptons exhorted her to brace up and take comfort, she would not.

At the end, she confirmed the Protestant faith in which she had been brought up, saying that *'[she] believe[d] to be saved by the death of Christ.'* She then sent a last request to the Queen, to hold her children blameless for her own offences, and to ask Elizabeth to set Hertford free. To her husband, for so she was certain that he was, she left the diamond betrothal ring, her wedding ring, and a ring with a picture of herself set in it. Katherine died on 27th January, 1568, at the age of twenty-eight.

Elizabeth made a polite show of sorrow, and ordered a suitably grand funeral, complete with Katherine's arms of England, quartered with France, differenced for her descent. A sum of £140 was sent to Hopton for Katherine's final expenses and the costs of the funeral. Katherine was buried in the parish church of Yoxford, rather than in Westminster Abbey with her mother.

Hertford, surprisingly, seems to have learnt little from his experiences. Although after Katherine's death he was released and restored to the normal activities of a peer of the realm, he made two further secret marriages and had another couple of sojourns in the Tower.

After the accession of James I, Hertford managed, in 1608, to track down the clergyman who had married him to Katherine. It seems extraordinarily unlikely that the man, who had not come forward previously, should both still be alive, and identifiable. A suspicious mind might think that either Hertford knew where he was all along, or that he found someone willing to play the part. Nevertheless, there he was, prepared to swear that Hertford and Katherine had been legally married.

The incentive may have been his grand-son's secret plan to marry the Lady Arbella Stuart, who had a strong claim to the throne. Hertford died in 1621, having outlived Katherine by over 50 years. Their grandson had Katherine's body exhumed, and she now rests, finally at Hertford's side, in a grand tomb in Salisbury Cathedral.

Aspects of Lady Katherine Grey's Life

Chapter 15: Following the Footsteps of Katherine Grey

Katherine's childhood was typical of the nobility of the time – regular visits to London and the court, long summer months in the country, and a round of visits to family and friends. Unfortunately, she also spent a third of her life as a prisoner – first in the Tower of London, and then under house arrest in Essex and Suffolk.

The numbers in the text below correspond to those on the map which follows.

*

Katherine Grey was probably born at her parents' town house in London. Dorset House (1), in the City of London. Originally Salisbury Court, and the possession of the Bishops of Salisbury, Dorset House was located near the current City Thameslink station, clues to its location being in the names of Salisbury Court and Dorset Rise.

As well as their town house, the Dorsets owned Bradgate House (2) in Leicestershire. Building at Bradgate began around 1499 under the aegis of Thomas Grey, 1st Marquess of Dorset, Katherine's great-grandfather, who was the son of Queen Elizabeth Woodville, by her first marriage. The house, built in the fashionable, and expensive, red-brick favoured by the Tudor elite, was completed around 1520. Although it was not a small property, it was more in the nature of a country house, than a great mansion or castle. The remains of the house are still visible today.

During Katherine's girlhood, she would have spent a good deal of time here, particularly in the summer when nobles left London to avoid the diseases that tended to spread in the warmer months. During the hunting season, too, the Dorsets would spend time here – Leicestershire was (and is) considered one of the prime areas for hunting in England, and the vast parks surrounding the house would have been stocked with deer.

Part of aristocratic life was visiting relatives and friends. Katherine frequently visited the Willoughbys of Wollaton who were her paternal relatives. Lady Anne Grey, Lady Willoughby (d. 1548), being her father's sister. The two families remained close. When Sir Henry Willoughby died fighting for the Crown during Kett's Rebellion in 1549, the young Willoughbys, Francis, Margaret and Thomas, were placed in the care of their mother's relatives.

Thomas Willoughby was placed with the Dorsets and the other two with Dorset's half-brother, George Medley, at Tilty (3) in Essex. This was another house frequented by Katherine. Formerly a Cistercian Abbey, just before its dissolution, the Abbot had granted Dorset's mother, Margaret Wotton, Marchioness of Dorset, a sixty-year lease of buildings and land. Although the matter was looked into – fraud being suspected in a lease granted when the monasteries were being dissolved - it was found to be a legitimate transaction. No traces are left of Tilty today, although the parish church where the family probably worshipped, remains.

Another house in Essex where Katherine visited at least once, was Beaulieu (4), or Newhall. This was the home of her mother's cousin, the Lady Mary, daughter of Henry VIII. Near Chelmsford, the palace was built by Henry VIII in the 1520s – a recent excavation by Channel 4's Time Team found significant remains of the construction, again in the fashionable red-brick. The property was then granted to George Boleyn,

Lord Rochford, brother of Queen Anne Boleyn, before reverting to the Crown and being given to the Lady Mary in 1537. A private school now occupies the site.

When Katherine's father was granted the Dukedom of Suffolk, on the death of both her half-uncles in 1551, the family inherited a grand new town house, Suffolk House. The property was formerly Norwich House, the town house of the eponymous bishop, but was frequently used by courtiers. In 1528, it was suggested as an appropriate lodging for Cardinal Campeggio who had come to hear Henry VIII's annulment case. However, the idea was rejected because

> *'that lewd knave Jamys that nevyr did good hath so paynted Norwyche place to the Cardynall that it seemyth that logyng hym ther ye wold have logyd him in a pygge stye.'*

In 1536, this *'pig-sty'* was granted to Katherine's grand-father, Charles Brandon, Duke of Suffolk, in exchange for a house he had at Southwark. It reverted to the Crown following the execution of Katherine's father, and was variously used by Archbishops of York, the Lords Keeper, and even the Earl of Essex. No trace of the house remains today.

Another house, similarly located on the Strand, leading down to the Thames that Katherine would have known, was Durham House (6). Again, the palace of a Bishop, it was frequently used in the sixteenth century by royalty. Katharine of Aragon was lodged there during her widowhood, and Edward VI lived there before acceding to the throne. Under Henry VIII's will, it was granted to his daughter, the Lady Elizabeth, but the Duke of Northumberland contrived to wrest it from her, but not without her *'conceyvinge some displeser'* against him.

For Katherine, it was a significant location as the place where she was married to Henry Herbert, son of the Earl of Pembroke, on 25th May 1553.

Following her marriage, Katherine went to live at Baynard's Castle with her in-laws. Baynard's Castle had been the London home of Cicely Neville, Katherine's great-great-grandmother during the reign of Edward IV. In 1509, it was granted to Katharine of Aragon, and also formed part of the jointure of Anne of Cleves, on her marriage to Henry VIII. On Henry VIII's death it was granted to William Herbert, 1st Earl of Pembroke, and his wife, Anne Parr, sister of Queen Katherine. Katherine Grey was only resident here for a few weeks, as, following the failure of the coup intended to put her sister on the throne, Pembroke disowned the marriage, and sent her back to her mother.

Katherine spent the next few years as maid-of-honour to the new queen, Mary I. She would have lived at Whitehall, Greenwich, Hampton Court, Richmond and St James' Palaces, amongst other royal properties. She was present at the marriage on 25th July 1554 of Mary and Philip of Spain at Winchester Cathedral (8).

During the summer of 1558, Katherine spent several weeks at the manor of Hanworth. This was another royal property – it had been one of the dower houses of Katherine Parr. In the 1550s, it was occupied by Anne Stanhope, Duchess of Somerset. The Duchess, despite being a strong adherent of reform, and the widow of Protector Somerset, had always had a good personal relationship with the Queen Mary, and her daughter, Lady Jane Seymour, was another of the Queen's maids-of-honour, and Katherine's best friend.

The two girls were at Hanworth for Jane to convalesce after a bout of influenza that had almost carried her off. Katherine was courted by Jane's brother, Edward Seymour. On returning to court, the girls found that, whilst Jane had recovered from the influenza which, the Queen had now caught it, and had no hope of recovery. Katherine would have been at the Palace of St James where Mary died, and attended her funeral at Westminster Abbey in December 1558. In the following year, she attended her mother's funeral, also in the Abbey. Duchess Frances had spent her last years in her home at Sheen (9), near modern day Richmond-on-Thames.

Katherine remained at court under the new queen, Elizabeth I, although Elizabeth had far less time for her than Mary had had, and demoted her from the Privy Chamber. In due course, Katherine's romance with Edward Seymour (now Earl of Hertford) was rekindled, and in late 1560, aided and abetted by her friend Jane Seymour, the couple were secretly married at his house at Cannon Row, Westminster (10).

On discovery of the match, the wrathful Elizabeth clapped both Katherine and Hertford into the Tower of London (11), where they remained until the summer of 1563. When plague broke out, Elizabeth was persuaded to send Katherine, still as a prisoner, to her uncle, Lord John Grey's, home at Pirgo (12) in Essex.

Because Lord John was considered too lenient, and was also suspected of involvement in John Hales' book promoting Katherine's rights of succession, she was moved to Ingatestone Hall (13) under the care of Sir William Petre. Ingatestone Hall remains, a wonderful Tudor house that is frequently host to Tudor re-enactments.

Before too long, Katherine was on the move again, this time to Gosfield Hall, Essex, home of Sir John and Lady Wentworth, distant relatives of Hertford's. The property, built in the late 1540s, still remains standing and is used as a wedding venue. On the death of the elderly Sir John, Katherine was moved to what would be her final home-cum-prison, Cockfield Hall (14) in Suffolk.

Cockfield Hall still exists, although the building has been refurbished and is in largely eighteenth century style. Here, although her custodian, Sir Owen Hopton, did his best to restore her to health, Katherine succumbed to illness, exacerbated by depression and died in 1568.

Originally buried in the parish church at Yoxford, she was moved fifty years after her death to lie beside Hertford in and elaborate tomb in Salisbury Cathedral (15).

Key to Map

1. Dorset House, London
2. Bradgate, Leicestershire
3. Tilty, Essex
4. Beaulieu, Essex
5. Suffolk House, London
5. Durham House, London
6. Baynard's Castle, London
7. Hanworth Manor, London
8. Winchester Cathedral, Hampshire
9. Sheen, London
10. Cannon Row, London
11. Tower of London
12. Pirgo, Essex
13. Ingatestone Hall, Essex
14. Cockfield Hall, Essex
15. Salisbury Cathedral

Chapter 16: Book Review

The succession crisis of 1553, when her sister, Jane, briefly held the throne, is important in the story of Katherine Grey. Coverage of the events around the crisis was given a new twist by the late Professor Ives.

Lady Jane Grey: A Tudor Mystery

Author: Professor Eric Ives

Publisher: Blackwell Publishing Ltd

In a nutshell Professor Ives' contention is that, far from Lady Jane Grey being an innocent victim of a plot by those around her to usurp the throne, she was, in fact, the legitimate heir.

The late Professor Eric Ives is an historian of renown, some of whose other works I have thoroughly appreciated, so I was very curious to read this book. Professor Ives' central tenet is that far from being an attempt at usurpation, the accession of Lady Jane Grey in 1553 was a case of the Crown passing to the legitimate heir, and that her overthrow by Mary was the result of rebellion. This is not, of course, the received opinion, and I was eager to be convinced by new information or arguments. The '*mystery*' of the book is how such an overthrow was achieved.

The format of the book, too, is slightly unconventional, in that rather than a narrative of events, he begins by describing each of the main protagonists in detail. This is very helpful, as it prevents lots of asides when the main action of the book is presented. Unfortunately, Ives' predilection for Jane Grey results in a number of repetitions of incorrect facts and misogynist comments about Mary. For example he claims that

Mary's mother, Katharine of Aragon, encouraged her to see herself as *'half a Hapsburg'*. Neither Katharine nor Mary had any Hapsburg blood whatsoever. Nor is a description of Mary, aged 37, as *'ageing'* likely to have been used of any male in the story. In fact, he refers to Northumberland's achievements at *'barely forty'* as *'unique in Tudor England.'*

Passing on to Edward VI, the information about the development of Edward's authority, and how he moved from being a spectator in government, to beginning to formulate policy, is very persuasive. In particular, the detail about the development of the Devise for the Succession is comprehensive, although I found the statement that Edward *'never even thought of his half-sisters'* as possible heirs bizarre. Of course he must have thought of them, as they were named in his father's Will, and, in any event, within a few paragraphs Ives writes that Edward was deliberately creating a Will that *'mimics Henry VIII's own.'*

Ives then goes on to consider the legality of Edward's Devise. He first states that Parliament hadn't *granted* Henry VIII the right to change the succession, because that would suggest that Parliament was of higher authority than the King, not the position in the sixteenth century constitution, but merely recognised Henry's right. Thus, if Henry VIII had the right to change the succession by Will, so had Edward VI. I am not entirely convinced by that argument, as, although Parliament was not above the King, it was not necessarily the case that the King was above the law, although this was undoubtedly a murky area, not tested until the Civil War. It also does not accord with the wording of the act, which says:

'by the authority of the same (the Lords Spiritual and Temporal and the Commons) your highness shall have full and plenary power... to give, dispose etc.'

However, Ives establishes, to his own satisfaction, that Edward's Devise for the Succession document was legal and thus, the proclamation of Jane as Queen on Edward's death was fully justified, and totally in accordance with Edward's wishes. This raises the other plank of Ives' argument, which appears to be a complete exoneration of the Duke of Northumberland from any responsibility for the matter at all.

Ives contends, first, that the three marriages of May 1553 between Northumberland's son and Lady Jane, Pembroke's son and Lady Katherine Grey, and Northumberland's daughter to the son of the Earl of Hastings, were no more than the usual aristocratic arrangements. He even goes so far as to say that *the evidence is that the initiative for Jane's marriage did not come from Northumberland at all,* and that suspicion about Northumberland's motives was a post-event justification. He also adduces evidence that the other Privy Councillors were equally involved, although whether they were genuinely inclined to accept Edward's Devise, or brow-beaten by Northumberland as they claimed, is debated. Ives' view being that of Mandy Rice Davies in the Profumo Affair – *Well, they would say that, wouldn't they?*

Having identified that there was widespread support for Edward's Devise, Ives claims that this support was forthcoming because Henry's attempt to settle the Crown on illegitimate off-spring was a subversion of common law that had made all property owners uneasy, and thus the choice of Lady Jane as successor was entirely consistent with a return to the rule of law. Unfortunately, he does not then address the question of why, if common law should be followed, Edward's heir was not Mary, Queen of Scots? Or Henry Stuart, Lord Darnley? Even Lady Frances, rather than her daughter? All three of them would precede Jane Grey under common law.

Moving on from the legal issues, Ives addresses the events themselves, from the perspective that Mary's refusal to accept Jane as

Queen was an act of rebellion. The clear inference he draws is that the Privy Council just could not encompass the thought that Mary might rebel and therefore did not prepare thoroughly to circumvent it, rather than that they themselves were half-hearted. He also postulates that there was little objection to Jane's accession amongst the nobility or gentry, or even the population of London. He also disputes accounts that Northumberland had difficulty raising men.

This interpretation paints Ives into a corner. If everyone who counted supported Jane, and the commoners were happy to serve in her army, where did it go wrong? It wasn't even the defection of the six ships sent to patrol the Suffolk coast, and the dispatch of their guns to Mary, which is often postulated as the root of her success.

Instead, Ives sees the collapse of Jane's support as the fault of the Earls of Arundel and Pembroke who would not take military action themselves. The final section of the book deals with the aftermath of the crisis.

Whilst I hesitate to criticise such an eminent historian as Professor Ives, I cannot help but feel that the arguments in the book lack a certain level of logical integrity and don't necessarily follow from the information presented. The mystery is not really solved. Nevertheless, in spite of my reservations, I would recommend the book as a detailed account of the events of the summer of 1553.

Bibliography

Calendar of State Papers: Domestic Series: Edward VI, 1547-1553. United Kingdom: Stationery Office Books.

Calendar of State Papers: Domestic: Mary I 1553-1558. London: Public Record Office.

Calendar of State Papers Simancas, British History Online (HMSO, 1892) Hume, Martin A S, ed.,

Calendar of State Papers: Venice <http://www.british-history.ac.uk/cal-state-papers/venice/vol2/vii-lxi> [accessed 7 October 2015]

Cecil Papers, http://www.british-history.ac.uk/cal-cecil-papers (Accooood: 7 September 2015)

Letters and Papers, Foreign and Domestic, of the Reign of Henry VIII: Preserved in the Public Record Office, the British Museum, and Elsewhere in England (United Kingdom: British History Online, 2014) https://www.british-history.ac.uk/letters-papers-hen8/ Brewer, John Sherren, and James Gairdner,

Borman, Tracy, *Elizabeth's Women: The Hidden Story of the Virgin Queen*, Kindle (London: Jonathan Cape, 2009)

Childs, Jessie, *God's Traitors: Terror and Faith in Elizabethan England* (United States: Oxford University Press, USA, 2014)

De Lisle, Leanda, *Tudor: The Family Story* (United Kingdom: Chatto & Windus, 2013)

De Lisle, Leanda, *The Sisters Who Would Be Queen the Tragedy of Mary, Katherine, & Lady Jane Grey* (Glasgow: HarperCollins e-books, 2008)

Doran, S. *Elizabeth I and her Circle* 1st edn. (Oxford: OUP, 2015)

Doran, S. *The Tudor Chronicles.* (London: Quercus Publishing Plc, 2008)

Durant, David N. *Bess of Hardwick: Portrait of an Elizabethan Dynast,* 1st edn (London: Weidenfield and Nicolson, 1977).

Ellis, Henry, *Original Letters, Illustrative of English History: Including Numerous Royal Letters: From Autographs in the British Museum, the State Paper Office, and One or Two Other Collections.,* 1st edn (New York: Printed for Harding, Triphook, & Lepard, 1824)

Fletcher, A. and Vernon, L. (1973) *Tudor Rebellions (Seminar Studies in History).* 2nd edn. Harlow: Longman.

Foxe, John, *The Acts and Monuments of John Foxe: A New and Complete Edition: With a Preliminary Dissertation by the Rev. George Townsend* (London: R.R. Seeley and W. Burnside, 1837)

Hoby, Sir Thomas, *The Travels and Life of Sir Thomas Hoby Kt of Bisham Abbey, Written by Himself 1547 - 1564,* ed. by Edgar Powell (London: Royal Historical Society, 1902)

Holinshed, Raphael, *Holinshed's Chronicles of England, Scotland & Ireland* (United Kingdom: AMS Press, 1997)

Ives, Eric, *Lady Jane Grey: A Tudor Mystery,* 1st edn (United Kingdom: Wiley-Blackwell (an imprint of John Wiley & Sons Ltd), 2012)

Lemon, Robert, ed., *Calendar of State Papers: Domestic Series: Edward, Mary and Elizabeth,* British History Online (London: HMSO, 1856)

Sidney, Philip, *'Jane the Quene': Being Some Account of the Life and Literary Remains of Lady Jane Dudley, Commonly Called Lady Jane Grey* (London: Swann, Sonneschein and Co., 1900)

Strickland, A. and Strickland, E. (2011) *Lives of the Queens of England from the Norman Conquest: Volume 3 & 4.* United Kingdom: Cambridge University Press (Virtual Publishing).

Strype, John, Annals of the Reformation and Establishment of Religion and Other Various Occurrences in the Church of England Etc. (Oxford: Clarendon Press, 1824),

Tremlett, G. (2010) *Catherine of Aragon: Henry's Spanish Queen.* London: Faber and Faber.

Warnicke, R. M. *Wicked Women of Tudor England: Queens, Aristocrats, Commoners* (New York, NY: Palgrave Macmillan, 2012)

Weir, Alison, *Elizabeth, the Queen,* Kindle (London: Random House UK, 2009)

Whitelock, Anna, *Elizabeth's Bedfellows*, Kindle (London: Bloomsbury Publishing plc, 2013)

Whitelock, Anna, *Mary Tudor: England's First Queen*, Kindle (London: Bloomsbury Publishing plc, 2010)

www.tudortimes.co.uk

47216390R00033

Printed in Poland
by Amazon Fulfillment
Poland Sp. z o.o., Wrocław